The Colonial Williamsburg
COLORING BOOK

The Colonial Williamsburg Foundation
Williamsburg, Virginia

Sixth printing, 1992
ISBN 0-87935-052-0

Drawings by Vernon Wooten
Printed in the United States of America

James Geddy, Williamsburg's best known silversmith, lived in a house next to his shop.

Tasty food is prepared in the kitchen.

The blacksmith hammers an iron chain into shape.

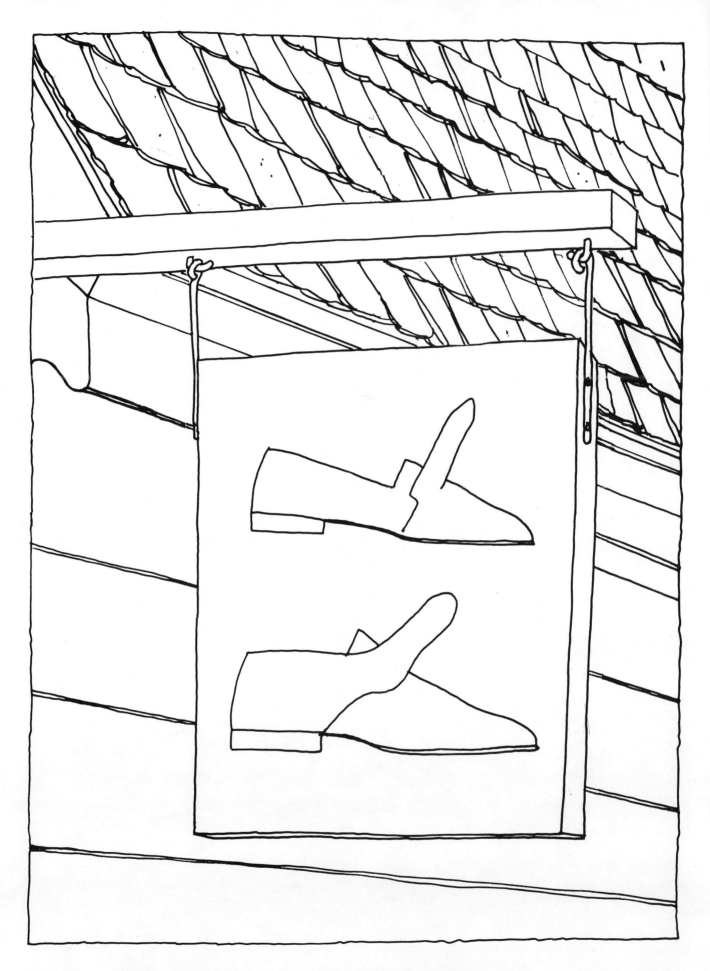

This sign advertises the articles that are sold inside the Shoemaker's Shop.

The speckled bird perches near its bird bottle house.

The basketmaker weaves baskets of all shapes and sizes.

Josiah Chowning's Tavern serves delicious food and drink.

The Great Union flag waves in the breeze above the Capitol.

Elegant dances were held in the Apollo Room at the Raleigh Tavern.

In Williamsburg, a baker makes bread and cookies.

A pair of oxen pull the two-wheeled cart.

A little boy greets a friendly Williamsburg colt.

Weapons and ammunition are stored in the Powder Magazine.

The silversmith carefully makes a silver bowl.

Musicians in costumes play in the Governor's Palace Ballroom.

The skillful cooper makes wooden barrels and kegs.

Seven royal governors lived in the Governor's Palace.

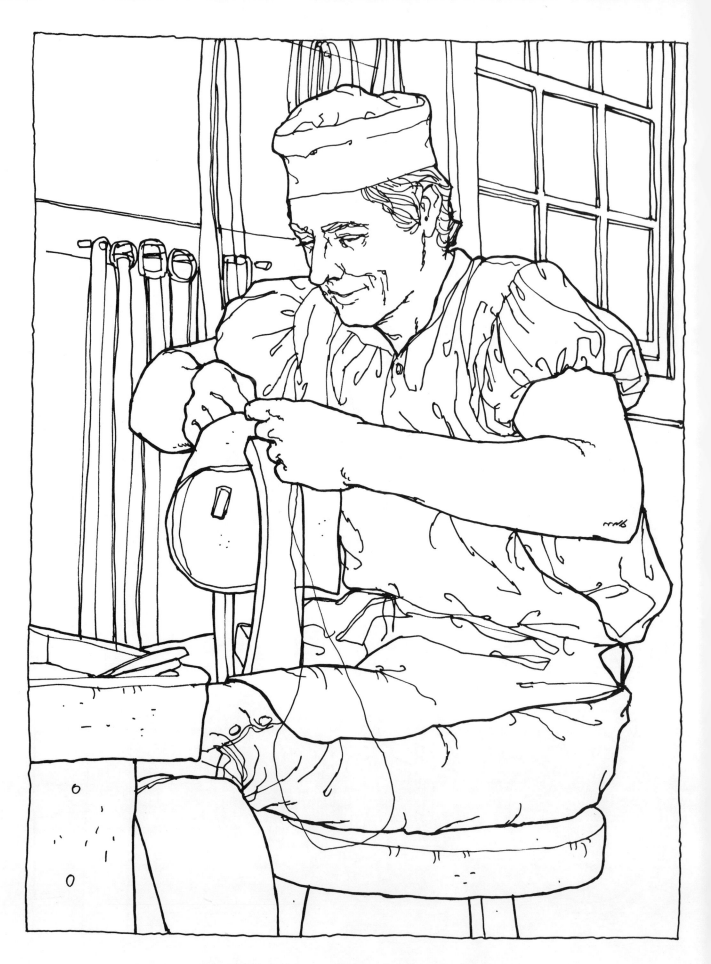

The harnessmaker sews harnesses and saddles.

The colonists worshipped at Bruton Parish Church.

A skilled craftswoman weaves cloth on a loom.

In the spring, gay tulips bloom in Williamsburg gardens.

Sometimes the cabinetmaker repaired violins or other musical instruments.

The milliner sold the latest fashions from London.

At the Windmill, the miller grinds grain to make flour.

Young ladies learned to play the harpsichord in colonial days.

Lawbreakers were locked in the pillory or stocks.

The gunsmith carves a design on the stock of a gun.

On the Palace Green, children enjoy petting the sheep.

The Apothecary Shop was the drugstore of colonial times.

Horse-drawn carriages go up and down the streets of Williamsburg.

The Courthouse, on busy Market Square, was the center of local government.

The Colonial Williamsburg Fifes and Drums march up and down Duke of Gloucester Street.

Colonial housewives spun wool into yarn on a spinning wheel.

Gentlemen were shaved and bought wigs at the eighteenth-century barbershop.